Skydiving

by Christopher Meeks

**Published By
Capstone Press, Inc.
Mankato, Minnesota USA**

Distributed By

CP CHILDRENS PRESS®
CHICAGO

CIP
LIBRARY OF CONGRESS CATALOGING IN PUBLICATION DATA

Meeks, Christopher.
    Skydiving / by Christoper Meeks.
        p. cm. – (Action sports)
    Summary: Describes the history, equipment, and techniques
of skydiving.

    ISBN 1-56065-051-6:
    1. Skydiving – Juvenile literature. (1. Skydiving.) I. Title II.
Title: Sky diving. III. Series.
GV770.M4 1989
797.5'6 – dc20   89-27877
                                     CIP
                                     AC

Photo Credits

Special thanks for the wonderful photographs by MICHAEL McGOWAN.

CAPSTONE PRESS
Box 669, Mankato, MN 56001

Contents

On the Edge

You Jump From An Airplane

The wind pushes at you like a hurricane. It whistles around your ears so you can hardly hear. The drone from the airplane's single engine adds to the noise level. However, you do hear the words, "Are you ready?"

You stand near the open door of the four-passenger Cessna airplane. Below you, far below, is the green-checkered land. You are higher than any building. One simple step and you could be out. You wear an orange nylon flight suit, gloves, goggles, comfortable shoes and a parachute.

A cord, known as a **static line**, runs from your parachute to a ring on the floor of the aircraft. When you jump, the static line will pull out your parachute. Your instructor wants to know if you are ready.

You want to say "yes," but you cannot help think that what you are doing is crazy. Why hurl yourself into the sky and fall like a rock? Is that fun? Yes, for many people it is fun. For a few moments you will be weightless, just like an astronaut circling the earth. Expert skydivers sometimes delay opening their parachutes up

to a minute and a half. They can move across the sky like flying squirrels. They can turn and do somersaults. They can hold each other's hands and feet and make shapes and letters for people below watching them. When their parachutes billow up, they will glide down to the earth gently like dandelion puffs.

You have already had five hours of instruction on the ground to prepare for this. Even so, your mouth is dry from fear. "Yes," you tell your instructor, "I am ready."

The pilot flying the plane turns down the engine so that the plane just idles and glides. The plane is moving about 70 miles per hour.

"Okay, step out," yells your instructor.

You step onto a small platform over the plane's landing wheel, holding onto a **strut** for balance. The wind really pushes at you now. It is all you can do to hold on. Your heart beats quickly, and you are breathing fast. You are getting a bit dizzy. "No, no, no," you tell yourself. "Stay calm. Breathe normally."

You hold the strut firmly with both hands and let your feet go. The wind pushes your body out at an angle, like a leaf on a branch.

"Go!" You hear from the plane, and you let go.

You spread your legs, arch your back and push your head back. The plane gets farther and farther away amazingly fast. You hear a "pop." That is your parachute coming out, but you do not feel anything. Your heart beats so fast, you can feel it in your neck. For a moment, you are confused – where is your parachute?

You remember the instructor saying that it takes a few seconds for the parachute to catch and balloon out. He said you would wonder where it was.

Then you feel a pulling. You look up. The beautiful striped parachute, also called a **canopy**, is full. It is a happy sight.

You do not feel as if you are falling, but the altimeter on your chest strap shows that you are getting lower. You are at 2,200 feet. A building would have to be 183 stories to be that high.

You reach for the two **steering toggles** above your head. By pulling on one or the other, you can control the direction of your movement. Pulling the one on the right, you turn right.

Looking down, you see a green-shingled barn and a red car parked near it. They look like toys, they are so small. The trees look like green cotton balls. The road looks like a thick line. You steer toward an open area because you want to stay

away from trees, power lines, fences, houses, buildings, lakes and pools and anything that can possibly be dangerous.

The barn to your left is getting bigger fast, and now you know you are moving down quickly. A grassy clearing is coming up.

When you are only about ten feet away, you pull down hard on both steering toggles. The parachute flares out and "brakes." It slows you almost to a stop. You lock your feet and knees together, keeping your knees bent. You land softly. It is as if you jumped off a small stool.

You look around – at the trees, the grass, the barn. Your hands are shaking, but that is normal.

A moment later, you hear something drop and you look over. Your instructor has landed, too, just behind you.

"Congratulations," he says.

From the Beginning

The First Skydivers

In 1797, Frenchman André Jaques Garnerin dropped from a balloon over Paris. He was strapped to a big silk canopy. He called it a

para-chute which translates roughly to "prevent-fall." Thousands watched his success. His parachute had no holes in the top to vent the air like modern chutes. Holes keep the chute from shaking. Because he had no holes, he had a bumpy ride down.

Before this, other people claimed to have parachuted, but no one saw these events. Leonardo da Vinci, the famous Italian painter and scientist, was perhaps the first to come up with the idea of air holding a person's weight. In 1495 he sketched a drawing of a parachute in his book Codex Atlanticus. He also sketched and made notes for a glider, a helicopter, and several other flying machines.

After Garnerin showed beyond a doubt that parachutes worked for people, more people tried it. Jumps became events at carnivals.

The first parachutes had to be open before a person jumped. The top of the chute was attached to the bottom of a balloon's basket. The jumper had to get in place under the basket and chute. The balloon's pilot would cut the line that held the parachute. The jumper would drift down.

Airplanes added a new problem for parachuting. They moved much faster than balloons. They flew 50 miles per hour or more across the sky. The fragile chutes used at that time would have been ripped to shreds in an instant by the force of the wind. So new designs were invented.

Grant Morton made the first parachute jump from a plane in flight in early 1912. He threw his chute up into the air, then leaped. Not all record books honor Morton's feat, however. Some credit the first airplane jump to Captain Albert Berry, who hopped from a plane with a chute that came out of a holder. That was in March, 1912. The next year, Georgia "Tiny" Broadwick, 20 years old, became the first woman to parachute from a plane. She had been parachuting from balloons since she was 15 years old.

At the end of World War I, the Germans began using the parachute. It was a great way to save a pilot's life when his airplane was crippled in a dogfight. The Allies later caught on to this, too. Parachutes moved from carnival shows to a valid use in emergencies.

Until 1919, many people felt that a parachute needed to open immediately after a person jumped. Otherwise, the jumper might black out from the continuous fall (**free fall**). It was thought the air would be sucked from a jumper's body and that he or she would be unconscious or dead in seconds. In 1919, however, Leslie Irvin strapped on a newly invented backpack parachute. It had a **rip cord** (a handle to open the parachute). He jumped from a plane traveling 100 miles per hour. He proved that a jumper could remain conscious and in control when the chute opened.

Aviation blossomed in the 1920s, and interest in parachutes also grew. The jump-and-pull backpack chute became common. It saved the lives of many people, including early flyer, Charles A. Lindbergh four times. By the end of World War II, parachutes had saved more than 80,000 lives.

Modern Skydiving

A skydiver is someone who chooses to free fall for many thousands of feet before pulling the rip cord. The first true skydiver was Steven Budreau in 1925. He jumped from a bomber at 7,000 feet. Then he pulled his rip cord at 3,500 feet.

Budreau and other free-fallers discovered that after falling about 1,500 feet, one's body tended to spin. If not corrected, or **stabilized**, then one would spin faster and faster and blackout. By moving one's arms and legs ever so slightly, spin can be stopped.

After 1925, jumpers tried higher and higher heights. Some went as high as 18,000 feet without using special equipment such as oxygen

tanks and pressurized suits. With special equipment, the record altitude for a parachute jump is 102,800 feet.

From the mid-1920s on, parachute design and reliability steadily improved. World War II created a new kind of soldier, the paratrooper. These were crack military men who jumped from airplanes, day or night. They were fully armed and prepared for action when they landed. Parachutes were also designed to allow the dropping of such military needs as cannons, trucks, food and ammunition.

Skydiving as a sport caught on after World War II, especially with paratroopers from the war who wanted to try jumping for fun. Parachutes have evolved from the heavy, round-canopy military chutes of the 1950s to the light, wing-shaped chutes used today. Now the "opening shock" of the parachute is smooth. Parachutes are steerable for better control. Over 2.25 million jumps are recorded each year in the United States. There are about 18,000 active skydivers in the country.

The Sport Today

Skydiving is strongly regulated by the Federal Aviation Administration (FAA). In addition, the sport is overseen by the United States Parachute Association (USPA). The USPA formed in 1967

from the Parachute Club of America. The world-governing body is the Federation Aeronautique Internationale. Its main office is in Paris, France.

While many people might consider skydiving crazy, people who do it over and over like it for the feeling of flying their own body. Tim Monsees of the Sky's West Parachute Center in Colorado said, "Some people are still scared after 50 jumps. For them their thrill and excitement outweigh the worry. That's what keeps them coming back."

The First Jump

Most skydivers have learned the sport by beginning with static-line jumps. A static-line jump is like the one described at the start of this book. A cord about eight feet long is connected to your parachute pack. The other end of the cord is anchored to the plane. When you jump, the line pulls your parachute out. You need to make 24 static-line jumps before you are permitted to free fall unassisted.

Until 1985, most first parachute jumps were the static-line kind. It was something you did alone. In 1985, however, the FAA approved the tandem chute. With only a little bit of training, a student can now experience free fall. The student is attached to a jumpmaster. The jumpmaster, an

expert skydiver, controls the fall and the parachute. People find this method less difficult.

Another kind of first jump is the **accelerated free fall** program. This is where two instructors hold onto you. They jump with you out of the plane, and they stay with you until you pull your rip cord. You need at least six hours of ground school to do this. You need eight accelerated free-fall jumps before you can free fall alone.

Automatic openers have added to the safety of the sport. They open your parachute if you forget. (Who can forget? You say. It happens, though.) Automatic openers were first developed by the military for emergency jumps and seat ejections. They work either with a timer or by using barometric pressure. They can open either the main or reserve chutes.

Conditions

Parachuting can be done just about anywhere there is open land. Normally, a telephone call to notify the FAA of one's plans will do.

Skydivers, cannot land just anywhere. They have to land where people do not mind or have given permission for the landing. The landing zone needs to be free of trees, wires, water, and moving objects.

In order to jump, you first need approved ground school training. The training takes about four to eight hours if you will be jumping out alone. It takes less than an hour if you will be jumping tandem, strapped to an instructor.

The training for solo jumping includes the basics of your exit. You also learn how to do the stable spread position with a strong arch to your back. You will cover emergency situations, how to pull your rip cord, how to steer your parachute, and how to land.

You cannot jump from just any plane. The airplane has to be one approved by the FAA. This is because the airplane's door must be open for jumpers. Only certain planes have the right kind of door and meet all the other qualifications for skydiving.

Among the many other regulations, you need to skydive in good weather. If the wind is too strong, you cannot jump. You also cannot jump through clouds. (You do not want to hit an airplane or another skydiver hidden in a cloud.)

All jumpers must jump with two packed parachutes: the main chute, and a reserve chute. The reserve is in case something happens to the main. Jumpers can pack their own main chutes. Only certified packers can pack reserve chutes. Reserve chutes must be repacked every 120 days.

The United States Parachute Association has a list of group member parachute centers. The centers follow the USPA basic requirements for student and advanced skydivers. The centers also offer first-jump courses. They are taught by USPA-rated instructors. At most centers, you need to be at least 18 years of age or older to jump. A few centers allow 16- and 17-year-olds to jump with written parental consent.

Equipment

For skydiving, all you need are coveralls, goggles, gloves, helmet, and an **altimeter**. You also need a parachute and a plane to take you up. The equipment (minus the plane) costs about $2,500 for each jumper. Most parachute centers have the items for rent. They also have skydiving packages that include training and an airplane.

Advanced Skydiving

Free-falling allows you to enjoy the fun of the sport. It takes 10-12 seconds to reach a speed of 100 miles per hour. Your position is controlled by how you move you arms, legs, hands and feet. When you reach your **terminal velocity**, you no longer feel the pull of gravity. This is because gravity is balanced by the wind resistance against your body. You are on top of a column

of air. It feels as if you are floating on a strong wind.

A wrong movement, however, can throw you into a somersault, spin or other uncontrolled maneuver. For your first free falls, you concentrate on stability and getting the feel of the air. When you get good, you might learn fancy moves called **aerobatics**.

The longer you fall, the more difficult it is to hold the rigid spread-eagle position. The experts relax. Their arms and legs are bent at 90 degrees. Control in this position is much easier.

Advanced skydivers like to be active in the air. They may be practicing aerobatics, much like a diver. They may do a barrel roll or twists and spins. If they jump with several others, they might try to meet in mid-air. In mid-air, they can make formations such as stars. Any maneuver that uses two or more people meeting in mid-air is called **relative work**.

Skydiving competitions generally have aerobatic events, relative work events, and jumping for accuracy. In jumping for accuracy, skydivers aim for a small round dish on the ground. It requires precision control of one's parachute. The other two events are judged on style and degree of difficulty.

Aerobatics

Aerobatics can range from simple turns to multiple twists and spins. Most advanced sky-divers just practice basic aerobatics: turns, front and back loops, barrel rolls, and the back-to-earth position.

There are three kinds of turns: foot turns, hand turns, and body turns. Foot turns are done by raising and lowering the feet and legs. Whichever foot is lower, the body turns that way. Hand turns are done in the relaxed position. You tilt your hands one way or the other and the body responds with a turn. A body turn simply involves twisting the body right or left. You lower one shoulder to turn that way. Body turns also usually use the arms and legs.

A back loop is a backward somersault. A front loop is a forward somersault. A barrel roll involves twisting around and then somersaulting. All these maneuvers happen in a split second.

Back-to-earth means you are falling on your back. You look up into the sky. It is the most relaxed position in free-falling, but requires concentration to avoid uncontrolled turns and spins. To get back into a face-to-earth position, you only need to arch your body and tilt your head back. It is the basic spread-eagle position. Almost any wrong move can be corrected by returning to a basic spread-eagle position.

Relative Work

Meeting people in mid-air looks easy and fun. In fact it is quite difficult. This is because of the speeds involved. There can be an 80 to 100 mile-per-hour difference. To fall side-by-side at the same speed takes experience.

Besides being able to fall side-by-side at the same speed, skydivers often need to move across the sky, like a glider, to meet. This is called **tracking**. A jumper may attain a tracking speed of up to 60 miles per hour. Caution needs to be used in tracking, too. A "bump" at 60 miles hour is a crash. A large number of accidents in the sport have happened because of mid-air collisions. Relative work must be executed carefully.

To make giant stars, one person remains stationary. The other people track toward them slowly. Because they move slowly and carefully to avoid bumping, the skydivers might not reach each other by the time they reach 3,500 feet. Between 4,000 feet and 3,500 feet is the altitude to move away from each other and pull the rip cord.

When people skydive together, everyone gets far away from each other when it comes time to open the parachutes. You would not want someone to drop on top of your parachute or to get your parachute tangled up with someone else's.

Canopy Relative Work

Until the late 1950s, parachute design had not changed much since the turn of the century. Most parachutes had round canopies. They opened quickly and caused a harsh jolt for the parachutist. The jumper then drifted down where the wind took him or her. The parachutes could not be steered.

Round canopies were then modified. They were given slots and holes which made them stearable. Sleeves were invented for the canopy so that the opening shock for the parachutist was reduced. It was less pain and more fun.

In the 1960s, more and more parachute designs came out. Some had square canopies. Others were triangle shaped. The designs offered more control. In the 1970s, a major new design came on the market. It was called a parafoil. It worked much like an airplane wing, creating lift. It could be "flown" like a glider. One could land light as a feather. These new parafoils allowed people to land softly and where they wanted to.

Because today's parachutes are so easily controlled, a new offshoot of the sport has developed. It is called **canopy relative work**. As in free fall relative work, jumpers connect themselves to each other. Instead of latching on side-

by-side, however, they stack themselves one on top of another. They look like multiple kites on the same string.

The interesting thing about canopy relative work is that the stacks are built from the top down rather than the bottom up. Each parachutist moves underneath the stack. The person on top grabs the parachute below.

Safety

The impressive safety record in the sport comes from following several simple and clear cut rules.

First, no one should skydive without adequate training. Every skydiver needs to understand all the physical forces involved. They need to know what to expect after jumping. Everyone must also know how to react when the unexpected happens. Almost all instructors are USPA certified, and most skydivers are licensed.

All reserve parachutes must be approved by the FAA. All parachutists must jump with two parachutes, a main and a reserve. (The exception is a tandem jump, where a student is strapped to an instructor. These two people as one unit, however, have two parachutes.)

Skydiving must be done in good weather and clear airspace.

A jumper avoids being over other jumpers, especially under 4,000 feet. This is because you do not want to plunge into someone else's parachute. When jumping with others, you give a wave-off signal just before opening your parachute to make sure everyone is away from you.

The United States Parachute Association stresses that parachutes must be deployed at 2,500 feet or higher when making a jump. (For experts, it is 2,000 feet.) This allows a person time to pull out the reserve chute.

When doing relative work, such as making stars, everyone must disband by 3,500 feet. The added height gives time for everyone to move away from each other. When doing canopy relative work (parachute stacking), everyone must finish docking or changing the formation by 2,500 feet. Collapsed canopies are not uncommon in parachute stacking. Above 1,000 feet, a canopy has time to reinflate.

There are other rules and guidelines, too, that you will need to learn if you take up the sport.

Getting Started

To learn more about skydiving and parachutes, you might go to a competition or a parachute center and watch skydivers in action.

Another way to learn is to read more about the sport. Your local library will probably have several books on the subject. You might also look for issues of a skydiving magazine. There are two magazines about skydiving:

Parachutists
1440 Duke Street
Alexandria, VA 22314

Skydiving Magazine
1050 Flight Line Blvd.
Deland FL 32721

If you would like a list of USPA group member parachute centers, you can write the organization at:

United States Parachute Association
1440 Duke Street
Alexandria, VA 22314

First jump packages cost anywhere from $100 to $175. They include training, equipment rental, and the airplane ride. Most schools now take first-timers on a tandem jump. If you want to get more involved in the sport after your first jump, join an accelerated free fall program. Such programs will cost $1,000 or more. You will make at least eight jumps, and you will have an instructor in the air with you (two instructors at first).

If you get really involved in the sport, the main costs will be to buy equipment. Once you buy your parachutes and flight gear, the cost of a ride up in an airplane ranges from $12 to $20 each jump. Your local parachute center will have the exact costs.

It takes a special person with definite needs for adventure to be a skydiver. It is certainly not for everyone.

Glossary

Accelerated Free Fall: A jump with 2 instructors holding onto the new jumper. The instructors hold on until the new jumper pulls his or her rip cord.

Aerobatics: Different skydiving positions like turns, front and back loops, barrel rolls and the back-to-earth.

Altimeter: A guage that measures altitude.

Automatic Opener: A device that opens a parachute automatically at a set altitude.

Canopy: The surface of an inflated parachute.

Canopy Relative Work: Jumpers who connect themselves to each other by stacking themselves on top of each other.

Free Fall: Falling through the air without the parachute being open yet.

Relative Work: Meeting other skydivers in mid-air while skydiving.

Rip Cord: The cord one pulls to open a parachute.

Static Line: A line connected to the airplane that automatically pulls open the parachute when a person jumps out of the airplane; used in place of a rip cord.

Steering Toggles: Lines on a parachute that control the steering of the parachute.

Strut: A brace on the airplane.

Terminal Velocity: The point at which the pull of gravity cannot be felt by a skydiver because gravity is balanced by the wind resistance against the body.

Tracking: A jumper moving across the sky, like a glider, to meet another skydiver.